P is for Prairie Dog

A Prairie Alphabet

Written by Anthony D. Fredericks and Illustrated by Doug Bowles

Text Copyright © 2011 Anthony D. Fredericks
Illustration Copyright © 2011 Doug Bowles

Sleeping Bear Press™

315 E. Eisenhower Parkway, Ste. 200
Ann Arbor, MI 48108
www.sleepingbearpress.com

Sleeping Bear Press is an imprint of Gale, a part of Cengage Learning.

First Edition

10 9 8 7 6 5 4 3 2 1

Library of Congress Cataloging-in-Publication Data

Fredericks, Anthony D.
P is for prairie dog : a prairie alphabet / written by Anthony D. Fredericks;
illustrated by Doug Bowles.
p. cm.
ISBN 978-1-58536-508-1
1. West (U.S.)—Juvenile literature. 2. Prairie Provinces—Juvenile literature.
3. Prairies—Juvenile literature. 4. Frontier and pioneer life—Juvenile literature.
5. Alphabet books. I. Bowles, Doug, ill. II. Title.
F591.F84 2011
978—dc22
2010030633
Printed by China Translation & Printing Services Limited, Guangdong Province, China.
1st printing.   11/2010

A a

Agriculture starts with A,
it's all the crops we grow—
corn, alfalfa, barley, wheat
in valley, field, plateau.

The prairies of the United States and Canada are often referred to as the Great Plains. A prairie is a treeless, grass-covered plain, rich in plant and animal diversity. Fertile prairie soil is also perfect for growing crops. Agriculture is the production of food through farming. Many prairie lands have rich soil that is perfect for farming. Early settlers thought it would be easy to farm in the prairies because they would not have to cut down trees to create farm fields. They discovered that the tough prairie sod was difficult to plow through. A blacksmith named John Deere made the first steel plow. Its highly polished blade was slick and sharp, which helped the farmers turn the tough prairie sod into fields of grain.

When settlers came to the prairies in the 1800s, wheat was a first choice because big tracts of land were available and it could be easily grown in the rich soil. Corn is another prairie crop that plays a significant role in our food supply. Corn is fed to dairy cows and chickens, and is used to fatten beef cattle and sweeten many food products. Barley, oats, alfalfa, and rye are other crops grown throughout the prairie region.

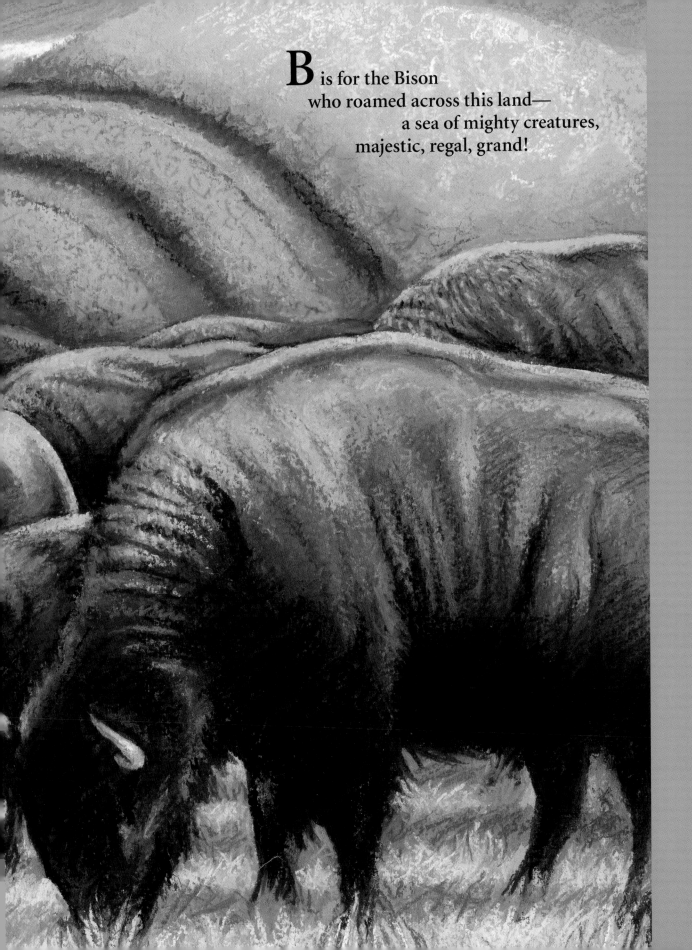

B is for the Bison
who roamed across this land—
a sea of mighty creatures,
majestic, regal, grand!

The bison is the biggest land animal in Canada and the United States. A male bison can weigh as much as 2,200 pounds (1,000 kg) and stand more than 6.5 feet (2 m) high. Hundreds of years ago, bison roamed by the millions across the North American continent. The herds were often so large that the ground trembled when they ran.

Native Americans and First Nations people depended on the bison for their survival. They used the bison for food, shelter, clothing, and more. As pioneers moved westward, they hunted the bison for its meat. But overhunting drove the bison nearly to extinction. By 1890 bison had almost disappeared from the plains.

B is also for Blizzards. In winter the temperature on the prairie can sometimes drop to lows well below 0 degrees Fahrenheit (-17° C) from summertime highs of more than 100 degrees Fahrenheit (38° C). Winter often brings huge, blinding snowstorms—blizzards that can close roads, businesses, schools, and even entire towns. The blowing snow quickly piles up in drifts higher than the roofs of houses.

Bb

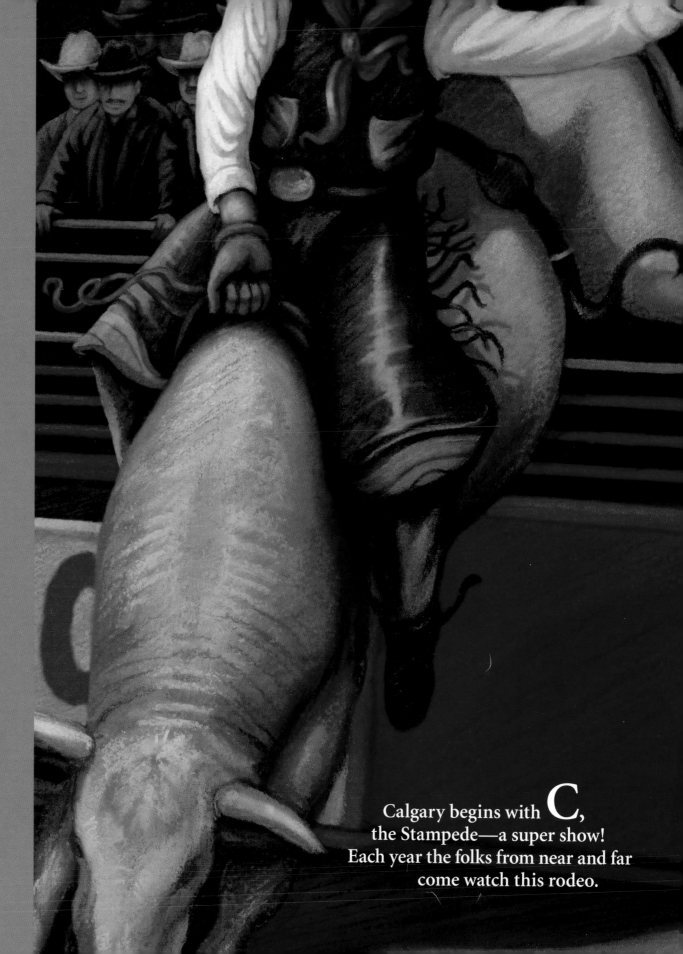

Alberta is one of Canada's three prairie provinces, along with Manitoba and Saskatchewan. Calgary is the largest city in Alberta, and it is the third-largest city in Canada, after Toronto and Montreal. It is located in an area of rolling foothills and high plains, close to the Rocky Mountains. This made it an ideal location for the 1988 Winter Olympics.

One of the most popular celebrations in Alberta is the Calgary Stampede, which bills itself as "The Greatest Outdoor Show on Earth." This ten-day festival and rodeo is held every July and attracts more than one million visitors a year. Bull riding, barrel racing, calf roping, steer wrestling, and the always popular chuckwagon races are some of the many events spectators have enjoyed ever since the first Stampede in 1912.

Calgary begins with C,
the Stampede—a super show!
Each year the folks from near and far
come watch this rodeo.

"The Dakotas" is a collective term for two northern states in the United States—North Dakota and South Dakota. These two states have many things in common including their geography, climate, animal and plant life, and heritage. Prairie areas include parks such as the Little Missouri National Grassland and Des Lacs National Wildlife Refuge in North Dakota and the Badlands National Park and Fort Pierre National Grassland in South Dakota.

Annual rainfall in this part of the United States averages 13–25 inches (33–64 cm) per year. Soil types range from thick black loam to porous sandy soils. In fact, soil scientists have identified more than 650 soil types in this region alone. As you might imagine, agriculture is a leading industry in both states. Common crops include corn, durum wheat, and sunflowers. There are approximately 31,000 farms in South Dakota and 30,000 farms in North Dakota. The average size farm is approximately 1,300 acres—that's pretty big!

D is for Dakotas,
both North and South are vast.
With fertile soil most everywhere,
the farming's unsurpassed.

Ecosystem starts with **E**.
It's plants and critters all
who mix and live together—
the large ones and the small.

An ecosystem is a natural area consisting of plants, animals, and micro-organisms all living together. Prairies are unique eco-systems dominated by grasses and other nonwoody plants. These ecosystems are the result of the interactions of precipitation (snow and rain) and temperature of a region, how quickly water drains from the soil, fire and flooding, and the effects of these things on plants and animals. Each plays a crucial role in the establishment of a prairie.

The lack of rainfall is important in the life of the prairie. Continuous grazing by bison, prairie dogs, and other animals also affects the growth of prairie plants. The grazing frequently stimulates new plants to grow. As animals graze, the action of their hooves sows seeds into the earth, helping to promote new vegetation.

Fire is also a necessary part of the prairie ecosystem. Fires, often started by lightning, may eliminate some old-growth trees while encouraging other plants to sprout. A mix-ture of young and old plants is always good in any ecosystem, including the prairie.

Here are some prairie facts:
- Prairies formed about 8,000 years ago.
- Prairies once covered about 40 percent of the United States; today only about 1 percent of wild prairies still exist.
- More than 100 plant species can be found in a prairie area of less than five acres.

As you travel across the prairie it seems hard to believe that at one time, about 70 million years ago, most of central North America was covered by an enormous inland sea. Here, large carnivorous fish swam, and *Tyrannosaurus*, *Triceratops*, and barrel-chested *Nodosaurus* roamed along the shallows of the sea. Slowly, over many millions of years, the sea disappeared and other creatures came to dominate this land.

Today, scientists are discovering the fossils of many different animals that once inhabited this region. The bones of ancient camels, rhinoceroses, large pigs, giant tortoises, and huge warthog-like mammals known as entelodonts have been unearthed by paleontologists. In places such as the Oglala National Grassland in Nebraska and the Pawnee National Grassland in Colorado, vast beds of prehistoric clams have been found by scientists and visitors alike. Crocodiles, ancient horses, mammoths, and saber-toothed cats are some of the other animals that once inhabited this region.

F is for the Fossils
of rhinos and dinosaurs.
They were the ancient beasts
that wandered ancient shores.

F f

More than 300 different species of grasses can be found throughout the prairie region. The area is divided into three general types: tallgrass, shortgrass, and mixed-grass prairies. Tallgrass prairies, with grass sometimes taller than a grown person, are home to a wide variety of plants and a rainbow of wildflower colors in the midsummer months.

The shortgrass prairies are long stretches of meadows sprinkled with an incredible variety of wildflowers such as daisies, violets, and junegrass. Many shortgrass prairie flowers blossom in the early spring, yet by midsummer most of the colors have faded.

The mixed-grass prairie is a wide belt of vegetation that runs southward from Saskatchewan through the Dakotas and down into Nebraska, Kansas, and Oklahoma. Here needle grasses and wheat grasses are most common, and sunflowers are one of the most recognized plants of this region.

G is for the Grasses,
the "mixed" and "tall" and "short."
They all are quite amazing
for wildlife they support.

H is for the Hawk
who soars through bright blue skies.
From distant cliffs and trees,
across this realm it flies.

Hawks are frequently seen flying above the prairie in both the United States and Canada. One of the best-known is the ferruginous hawk. These large birds have wingspans of more than four feet. They typically nest in trees, along low cliff faces, or on the ground. Ferruginous hawks can be distinguished by their white tails and broad white breasts. These birds feed primarily on prairie dogs, cottontails, and jackrabbits.

One of the most beautiful sights on the prairie is a large flock of Swainson's hawks, especially as the birds soar across the sky. These dark brown birds, slightly smaller than ferruginous hawks, feed on much smaller animals such as insects and rodents. Swainson's hawks are both graceful and elegant as they perform amazing aerial maneuvers high overhead.

H h

I i

I is for the Insects
that crawl and leap and hop—
like fireflies and locusts,
it seems they never stop.

North American prairies are home to thousands of insect species. These include more than 500 different kinds of butterflies, more than 200 species of grasshoppers, and nearly 10,000 species of beetles. Insects are important to the life of the prairie. They help loosen the soil, pollinate plants, and provide food for other animals.

Ants, moths, grasshoppers, crickets, dragonflies, and even tarantulas are scattered across this landscape. In the 1800s, enormous numbers of short-horned grasshoppers—called locusts when they swarm—would sometimes cover the sky, consuming everything in sight. Some of the largest swarms covered hundreds of square miles, with populations of several billions of locusts.

Illinois also begins with I. Illinois's nickname is "The Prairie State" although most of its tallgrass prairies are now gone. The largest remaining prairie in Illinois is Goose Lake Prairie State Natural Area south of Chicago.

Throughout the prairie, creeping juniper is a common plant. It grows low to the ground and often looks like a thick carpet of green spilling over rocks. Many Native American tribes used this all-purpose plant to cure illnesses. The twigs, leaves, and berries were used to create medicines that eased stomachaches, sore throats, fevers, toothaches, and hiccups, and even to help reduce the effects of smallpox and measles.

Native Americans also used juniper berries to flavor many foods. Even today, juniper berry sauce is a popular flavoring for many meat dishes.

Juniper begins with J—
what beneficial shrubs!
They cured diseases, fever, and colds
with berries, creams, and rubs.

Jj

K k

Kansas—it begins with K.
It is "The Sunflower State."
From fields of grain to cattle farms,
it fills our dinner plate.

People have been farming in Kansas for thousands of years. Two thousand years ago native people were growing crops like lamb's quarters and knotweed, which are thought of as weeds today. One thousand years ago they began growing beans, corn, and squash. Farming is central to Kansas's economy, culture, and traditions. Kansas grows more wheat, sorghum, and sunflowers than any other state. It has been estimated that about one out of every five jobs in Kansas is connected to agriculture.

The eastern third of the state features rolling hills and large forests, while the western two-thirds of Kansas is generally flat. Some people say that Kansas is "flatter than a pancake" (that's pretty flat!).

In 1803 the United States purchased an enormous tract of land from France known as the Louisiana Purchase. President Thomas Jefferson wanted to know about the Native American tribes, botany, geology, and wildlife in this region. He appointed Captain Meriwether Lewis to lead an expedition, afterwards known as the Corps of Discovery, to explore this newest addition to the country. Lewis selected William Clark as his partner and they, along with 33 other men, set out on May 14, 1804, heading west. Their two-year journey was the first American overland expedition to the Pacific coast. The journey laid much of the groundwork for the westward expansion of the United States.

Laura Ingalls Wilder also begins with **L**. Mrs. Wilder wrote a well-known series of children's books, the *Little House* series, which depicted life on the prairie in the late 1800s. Her stories have been read by millions of children and were developed into a very popular television series, *Little House on the Prairie*, in the 1970s. Laura Ingalls Wilder's books introduced many readers to the hardships of prairie living, describing life as it was lived long before electricity, running water, or modern transportation.

L l

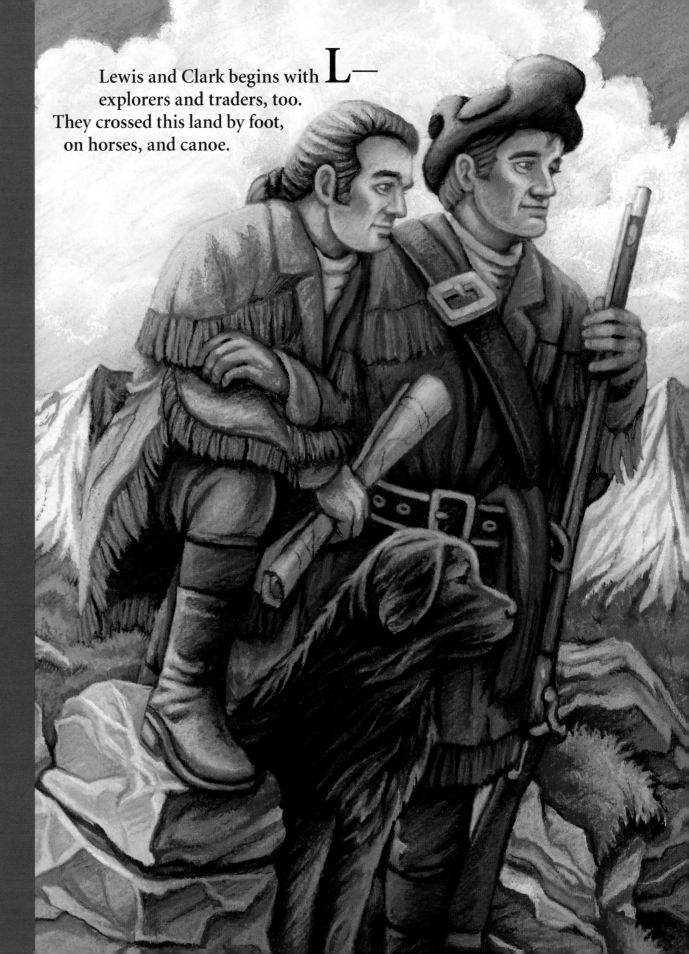

Lewis and Clark begins with L—
explorers and traders, too.
They crossed this land by foot,
on horses, and canoe.

M m

M is Manitoba,
a prairie province grand.
Rivers long and many lakes
are scattered through this land.

Manitoba is one of Canada's prairie provinces. Manitoba has more than 110,000 lakes, including the tenth-largest lake in the world, Lake Winnipeg. Most of the southern part of Manitoba is prairie, while the northern region is primarily forests. Most of the province's agriculture is based in the south, with cattle farming the predominant activity. Crops include grains, beans, oilseeds, and sunflowers.

N is for the Native people
who live across this land.
First people of the prairie—
Blackfoot, Sioux, Cheyenne.

Many anthropologists believe that the first inhabitants of North America were Paleo-Indians. These nomadic hunter-gatherers lived approximately 11,500 to 8,000 years ago. Later inhabitants built simple huts, hunted with bows and arrows, and tended gardens. From roughly 900 to 1880 "village farmers" (people of the Oneota culture) inhabited the central plains. They constructed large earthen lodges, stored food in pits, crafted jars and bowls, cultivated corn and beans, and hunted bison and other mammals. Some Plains Indians like Kiowa, Lakota, and Shoshone were nomadic (moving from place to place). Other tribes like Mandan, Pawnee, and Nez Perce were semi-sedentary (living in villages and raising crops).

When explorers ventured onto the plains they changed the lives of Native Americans and First Nations people forever. Tribes were displaced, bison herds were eliminated at a rapid rate, diseases such as smallpox were spread, and skirmishes flared up. Often tribes were confined to parcels of land known as reservations.

Today many Plains Indians continue living on reservations practicing aspects of their traditional cultures through art, music, literature, and film. Many tribes are working to improve social conditions on the reservations while maintaining the distinct identity of their tribal language and culture.

N
n

Omaha begins with O,
Nebraska's largest town.
Tall buildings, parks, museums—
a place of great renown!

O o

Omaha is the largest city in the state of Nebraska. During the 1800s, Omaha was an important transportation hub for pioneers traveling westward across the plains. Wagon trains headed to Oregon and California often began their journey in Omaha. Pioneers traveling west on the Missouri River also started in Omaha. And it was the point of eastern origin for the first trans-continental railway to be built across the plains. As a result of its location at the confluence of many road, rail, and water travel routes, this bustling city was often a starting point for early pioneers setting out across the wide prairies for the west.

Many immigrants who worked for the railroads and in the numerous meat packing plants made Omaha their home. Businesses supplying goods to the west and to the east were also based in this centrally-located city. Omaha was both a transportation and commercial hub and a "gateway" to the vast prairies that lay beyond.

The name prairie dog comes from the French *petit chien* (little dog) because this furry critter often barks in times of danger. Prairie dogs live in large colonies throughout the shortgrass prairies. Females have 1–6 pups each year. Prairie dogs are most active in the morning and evening hours, when it is cool. They live primarily on a diet of grasses, although they may occasionally eat small insects such as grasshoppers.

Prairie dogs typically live in underground towns of several thousand members—covering a hundred acres or more! They often poke their heads out of their burrows to survey their surroundings and scan for danger. Prairie dogs seldom wander far from the safety of their burrows.

P is for the Prairie Dog
who lives beneath the ground.
He scurries from his burrow
to peek and look around.

P p

Bob-white! Bob-white! Bob-white! The song of the northern bobwhite quail can be heard across the prairie in the spring and summertime. Males perch on fence posts or in haystacks and advertise their nesting sites to all the females in the area. Usually, bobwhite quail form pairs and nest on the ground. A single pair of quail can produce as many as twenty-five young during a single breeding season. During the non-breeding season, October through April, quail will gather together in larger groups (coveys) of five to thirty birds.

Quail have brown feathers, often speckled with black and white spots. This camouflage helps them hide from predators such as foxes, coyotes, raccoons, hawks, and owls.

Unfortunately, populations of northern bobwhite quail are declining in some areas due to a loss of food sources such as grains, fruits, and insects. Exposure during the harsh winter months, habitat destruction, and overhunting may also be factors contributing to their reduction.

Beginning with the letter Q
is Quail, a small, fat bird.
They call out to each other—
their song, it must be heard!

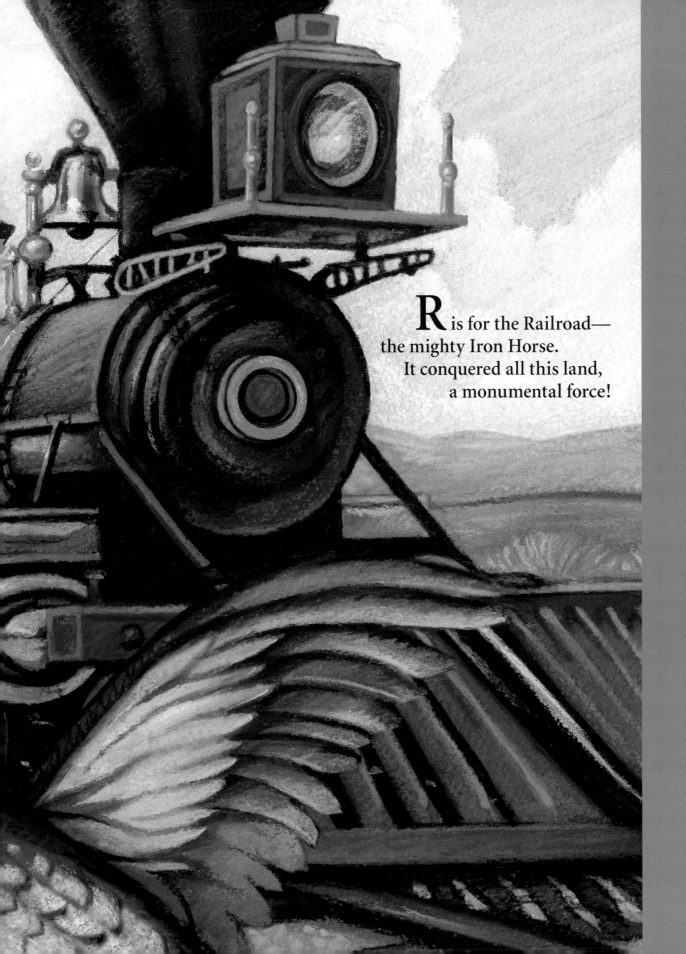

R is for the Railroad—
the mighty Iron Horse.
It conquered all this land,
a monumental force!

Building railroads was never easy. High mountains and deep valleys had to be crossed. Yet on May 10, 1869, the Transcontinental Railroad across the United States was completed, linking the eastern states to the Pacific coast. In the same way, the east and west coasts of Canada were linked in the late 1880s with the completion of the Canadian Transcontinental Railroad. Both rail systems helped people and goods travel more easily, cheaply, and conveniently. Today railroads crisscross the prairies in both countries, transporting people and goods across a vast and scenic landscape.

R r

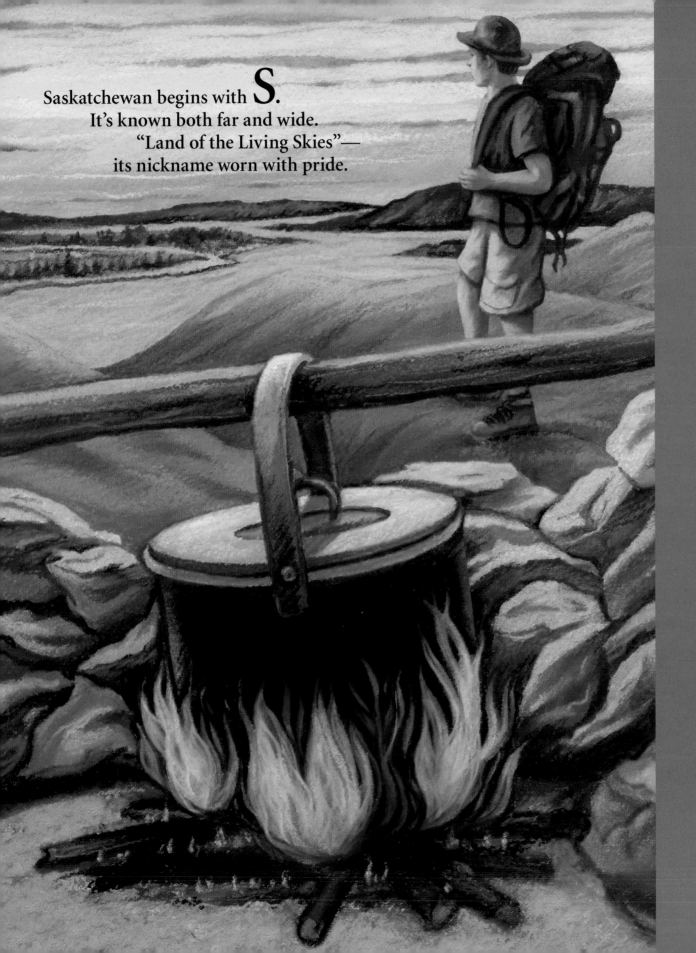

Saskatchewan begins with **S**.
It's known both far and wide.
"Land of the Living Skies"—
its nickname worn with pride.

Saskatchewan is known as "Land of the Living Skies." This refers to all the incredible weather patterns that appear overhead throughout the year. On cold winter days you may see rainbow arcs called sundogs on both sides of the sun. Strong winds and bone-chilling blizzards are also common during winter months. In the spring the sky is often clustered with a variety of cloud sizes and shapes. Be careful, though! This is also a time for tornadoes—those swirling funnels of wind that drop down out of the sky and sweep across the prairie. The heat of summer may bring booming thunderstorms, large hailstones, and remarkable rainbows. Autumn nights are often filled with the spectacular Northern Lights dancing across the sky. Each new season of the year brings new opportunity to get out and explore the Land of the Living Skies.

S is also for Soil. The soil under a prairie is a dense mat of tangled roots and bulbs. In fact, for most prairie plants two-thirds of each one is below the ground. Some roots die each year and decompose, adding organic matter to the soil. As a result, some prairie soils are rich, dark, and very fertile—great for farming. However in other areas where the climate is drier, particularly in the west, the soil may be dry and sandy—almost desert-like.

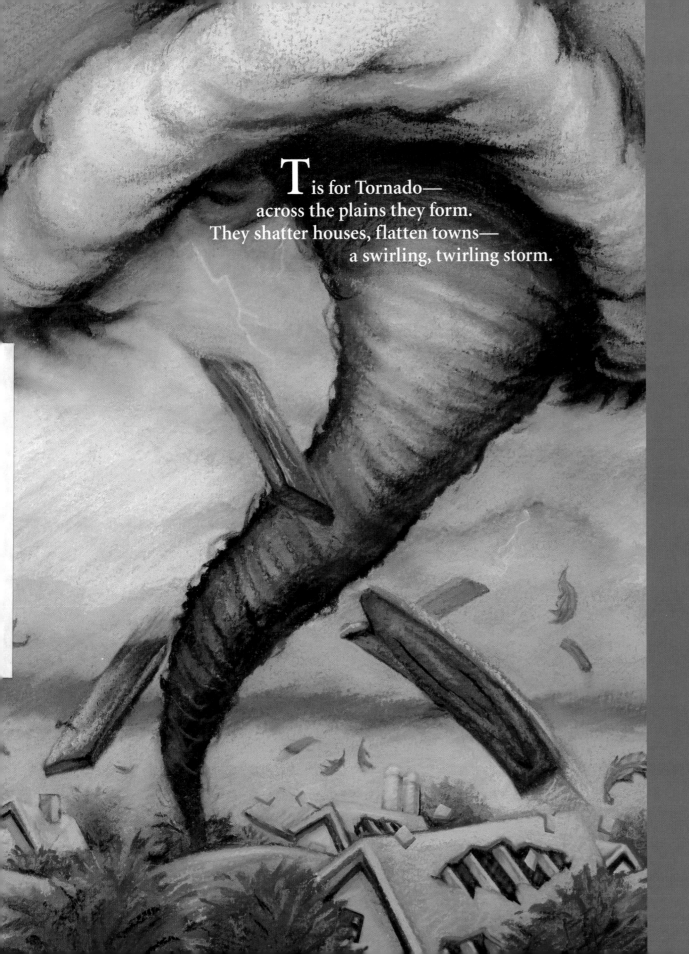

T is for Tornado—
across the plains they form.
They shatter houses, flatten towns—
a swirling, twirling storm.

Tt

Tornadoes are the smallest, most violent, and most short-lived of all storms. They occur almost exclusively through the North American prairies. This region of the country is often referred to as Tornado Alley.

Tornadoes usually occur during the spring and early summer. They often develop in the afternoon, when a layer of cold, dry air is pushed over a layer of warm, moist air. The warm air quickly forces its way in a spiral movement through the cold air and strong whirling winds form around a center of low pressure, producing a tornado.

Although tornadoes vary in size, they can be as much as one mile (1.6 km) wide. The winds within them can reach speeds of more than 200 mph (320 kph). Most tornadoes last for approximately eight minutes and travel about 15 miles (24 km). About 600–700 tornadoes are reported in the United States every year and frequently cause tremendous damage and destruction.

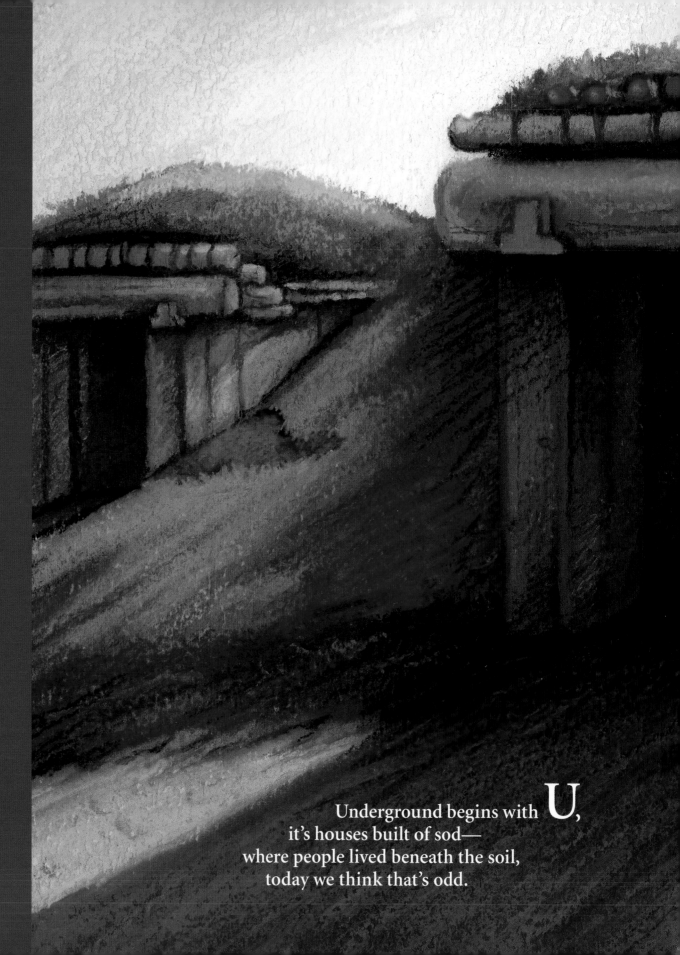

In 1862, during the American Civil War, the U.S. government passed the Homestead Act. This act offered pioneers free land if they could "prove up" their claim by living on the land and farming it for a certain number of years. When homesteaders arrived on the newly opened plains, there were not enough trees to build traditional log cabins, so they had to improvise. Family members dug a hole into a dirt bank and erected a roof of boards (pulled from their wagons) over-laid with sod. There they spent the first winter hunkered down underground. In the spring, when the winter snow melted, their "hole-in-the-ground" home often turned into a swamp.

Afterwards, many pioneers built a sod house. These were constructed of two-foot-wide (60 cm) "bricks" made from prairie sod. Sod houses were built above ground or into the side of a hill, often in a matter of weeks.

Typically, homesteaders lived five or six years in their "soddies." By then, they'd proved up their claim, taking title to 160 acres of land. They were also earning cash from their crops and livestock—money to buy wood and other materials for a real framed house.

U
u

Underground begins with U,
it's houses built of sod—
where people lived beneath the soil,
today we think that's odd.

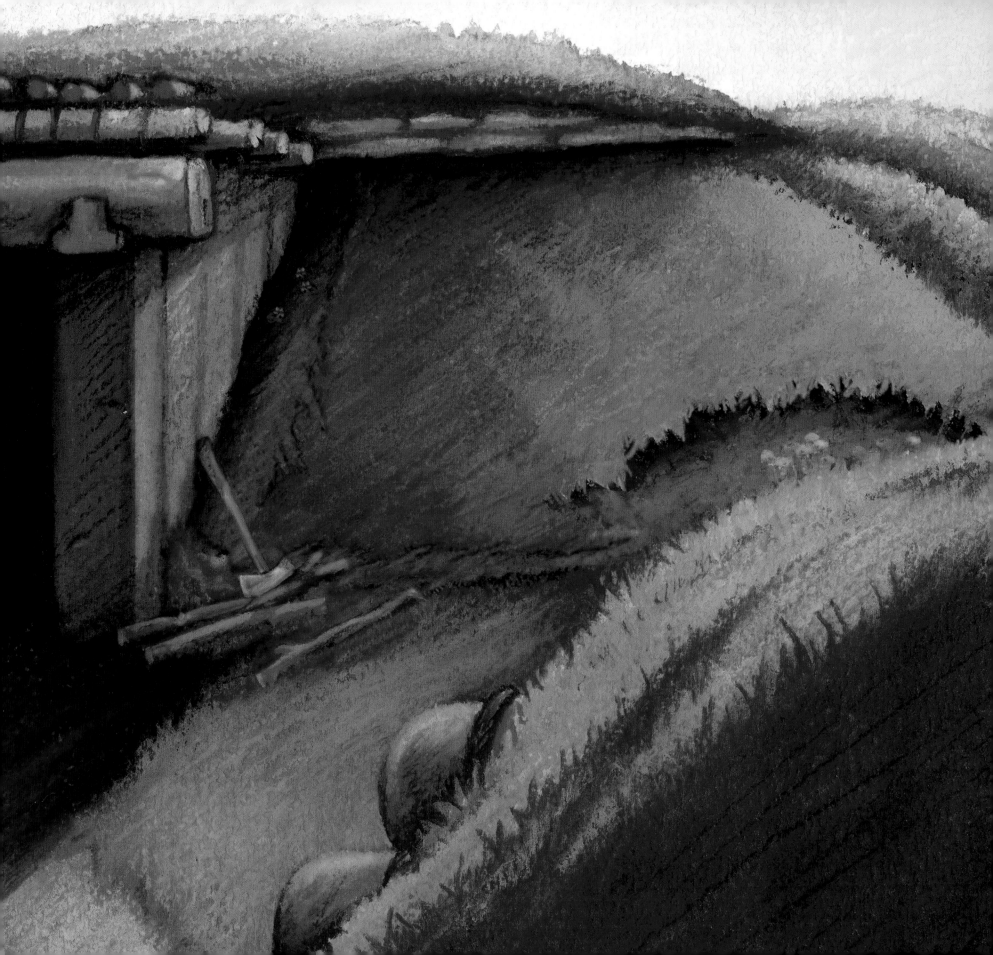

V v

V is for Vacation
across this wondrous land.
From rivers, fields, and mountains—
the scenes are always grand!

The prairies of North America are a popular tourist destination. For example, visitors can travel along part of the trail used by Lewis and Clark. They can watch a herd of bison at Tallgrass Prairie National Preserve in Kansas. They can explore the Badlands of the Dakotas, enjoy the beauty of the wild orchids of Saskatchewan and the blooming chollas of Texas, explore the riverside cliffs of Missouri, and follow the wind through the grasslands of Colorado's Front Range. They can walk through more than 160 species of prairie plants at the Living Prairie Museum in Winnipeg, Manitoba or discover long fields of corn in Iowa, Illinois, or Indiana. Wherever they go, tourists from near and far always find something to do, something to see, and something they will never forget when they visit a North American prairie.

In the United States, the prairie states include parts (or all) of Colorado, Illinois, Indiana, Iowa, Kansas, Minnesota, Missouri, Montana, Nebraska, New Mexico, North Dakota, Oklahoma, South Dakota, Texas, Wisconsin, and Wyoming. In Canada, the prairie provinces are Alberta, Manitoba, and Saskatchewan.

Anyone who has spent a few days on the prairie will tell you about the wind that seldom stops. Because the prairie has few trees and is mostly flat, the wind has very little to slow it down. During the drought years of the 1930s, parts of the southern plains were so dry that no crops would grow. Many trees and plants were cut down for farming and the bare fields had little to hold the dirt in place. As a result the dirt was whipped up into gigantic dust storms that spread for miles. The terrible storms of the Dust Bowl period forced many farmers to move away.

In winter a weather phenomenon known as Chinook winds often visits the eastern side of the Rocky Mountains. These winds are caused by moist air from the Pacific coast. The wind cools as it climbs the western slopes, then rapidly warms as it drops down the eastern side of the mountains. These warm winds are a welcome relief from the chilly winter temperatures.

W is also for Wheat. Thousands of farmers make their living growing wheat in the United States and Canada. More foods are made with wheat than any other cereal grain. One bushel of wheat contains about one million wheat kernels and will make about 67 standard-sized loaves of bread. An acre of prairie farmland can grow enough wheat each season to make 1,650 loaves of bread.

Wind begins with W.
It blows and blows and blows.
It whips 'round barns and silos
and over lines of clothes.

Xeric begins with X—
It's plants that only need
a little bit of water
to flower, grow, succeed.

X
x

Places that receive very little rain are sometimes known as xeric biomes (a biome is a community of plants and animals that live in the same area). The organisms that live in xeric areas have adapted to an arid or dry environment. Some plants you'd find there have spines instead of leaves. Spines significantly reduce the evaporation of water from these plants. They also keep the plants from being eaten by most animals. Other plants have long roots spreading out in all directions. When it does rain, these roots quickly gather up as much water as possible. Plants living in arid climates are known as xerophytes.

Animals, too, have adapted to this unique environment. Many of its creatures are nocturnal—they sleep during the day and hunt at night when the temperatures are cooler. They can also live on very little water since it may be weeks or months between rainstorms.

The western plains, where the Rocky Mountains limit the amount of rainfall, have the lowest level of precipitation (rain and snow) of the entire prairie region. Precipitation in the prairie can range from about 12 inches (30 cm) in the shortgrass prairie to about 22 inches (56 cm) in the tallgrass prairie.

Y is for Yellow,
 a color everywhere,
in flowers, fields, and sunsets—
 you'll always stop and stare.

Imagine fields of wheat stretching out to the horizon. Imagine a colorful rainbow after a sudden summer rainstorm. Imagine acres and acres of sunflowers sweeping over the countryside. Imagine the bright rays of the sun creeping through the trees or flowing down hills and over valleys. The color yellow is everywhere you look in the prairie.

Y also stands for Yucca. Yucca plants can be found throughout the prairie region and are well adapted to the environment. They have tough, sword-shaped leaves and produce large clusters of white flowers. Yuccas can only be pollinated by a single insect—the yucca moth. Yuccas are important since they help stabilize sandy soils, particularly in the western United States.

Long before European settlers discovered North America, hunting and trading parties of Native Americans and First Nations people traveled paths and trails over high mountains, through dense forests, and across long stretches of prairie land. Some of those trails followed paths used by animals as they wandered from one feeding area to another, or as they migrated from summer regions to winter homes. Those trails were used by many tribes as they moved, hunted, and traded throughout the region.

Later, as settlers explored and traveled westward, those same trails were used as convenient ways to get from east to west. They often wound around geographical barriers such as mountain peaks or led to swiftly flowing rivers. Sometimes they followed the natural contours of the land as they rose and fell with each valley and hill. Above all, they were a way for travelers to crisscross the prairie lands with some degree of comfort and safety. For many pioneers, these trails opened up unknown territories for exploration and settlement.

Z is for the Zigzag trails
that wandered east to west.
They brought the pioneers
who said, "This land is best!"

Zz

Q & A—The Prairie Way!

1. Which province has more than 110,000 lakes?

2. What insect travels in enormous swarms, eating everything in sight?

3. How fast can the winds in a tornado spin?

4. What animal was almost hunted to extinction by 1890?

5. Which is the largest city in the province of Alberta?

6. What animal lives in underground towns of several thousand members?

7. What crop has been grown throughout the world for almost 10,000 years?

8. What province produces 45 percent of Canada's grain?

9. Which state is known as the "World's Breadbasket?"

10. What plant was used by Native Americans to cure all sorts of ailments?

Answers

1. Manitoba
2. Locusts
3. 200 mph/320 kph
4. Bison
5. Calgary
6. Prairie dog
7. Wheat
8. Saskatchewan
9. Kansas
10. Juniper.